Through a Medium's Eyes

About Life, Love, Mediumship,
and the Spirit World

Rev. B. Anne Gehman

Volume 1

Through a Medium's Eyes Series

RUTH SHILLING

All One World Books & Media

Cover photo of B. Anne Gehman (2015): Ruth Shilling
Cover and interior designs: Ruth Shilling

ISBN : 978-1-9459630-1-8

Published by All One World Books & Media
West Kingston, RI, USA • all1world.com

Through a Medium's Eyes Series

All volumes are listed on page 97.

More Books by Ruth Shilling:

Color It True Series : Adult Coloring Books that Draw Good Things to You!

· *Marvelous Manifestation Mandalas, Vol. 1*
· *Magnetic Manifestation Mandalas, Vol. 2*
· *Miraculous Manifestation Mandalas, Vol. 3*
· *Angelic Manifestation Mandalas, Vol. 4*

Violin Success Series

· *SUCCESS with the Violin and Life: Strategies, Techniques and Tips for Learning Quickly & Doing Well*
· *Playing the Violin & Viola with VIBRATO* (ebook).
· *TONE: Violin & Viola Bowing Techniques for a Rich, Satisfying Sound* (ebook).

SINAI: *The Desert & Bedouins of South Sinai's Central Regions.* Published by Palm Press, Cairo, Egypt, 2003.

I dedicate this book to

my loving parents,

Johannes & Beatrice Gehman,

who gave me life

and to

Rev. Wilbur Hull,

who helped me understand my spiritual gifts

and how to be of service to others.

B. Anne Gehman

I dedicate this book

to my mom,

Carolyn Whitmore Shilling,

who started me off on this project

and to

all those in the spirit world

who love and inspire us.

Ruth Shilling

Table of Contents

Introduction   vii

CHAPTER 1. Who is B. Anne Gehman?   1

CHAPTER 2. Teachers & Mentors   15

CHAPTER 3. Guidance & Inspiration   23

CHAPTER 4. The Spirit World   31

CHAPTER 5. Mediumship   39

CHAPTER 6. Psychometry, Apports, Table   59
            Tipping and Remote Viewing

CHAPTER 7. Beliefs, Philosophies and   73
            the Power of Love

List of Stories   83

Anne's Recommended Reading List   85

Additional Resources   89

About the Author   93

List of Books in This Series   97

◆◆◆◆◆◆◆◆◆◆◆◆◆◆◆◆◆◆◆◆◆◆◆◆◆

Introduction

Story: Really?!

My mother passed to the spirit world in January 2013. I own and operate a tour business and was just about to leave the country for five weeks of tours in Egypt. With a slight delay for the funeral and legal arrangements, I landed in Cairo to begin leading our tours of the ancient sacred sites.

As I awoke each morning I felt my mom there with me, wishing me well on my day. Really?! It was the same gentle support and encouragement I had felt when with her in the past, but now here she *was* ("Is this possible?" I thought) right there in my hotel room in Cairo, and in my cabin on the cruise boat, and later in Luxor . . .

This was new for me. It was very clear it was my mom. But there was no physicality to it, just a feeling like I would have had if my eyes were closed and she was there in the room with me. I would *know* she was there. And there were words of supportive encouragement "sounding" in my head, too, a bit like remembering something someone said to me.

These visits were warm and embracing, and certainly left me feeling loved and supported, but I still felt grief about her having gone. However, it did open me up to a new possibility, the idea that our relationship *would* continue, though in a new and different way.

When I returned to the U.S., I got very interested in mediumship: what it is, how it works, who can do it ... I had lots of questions.

Twenty years earlier I had visited the Lily Dale Assembly in western New York and taught classes there in sound healing. Through doing healing and spiritual growth work, I had developed a vibrant and working relationship with the wonderful loving guidance that is our birthright.

At first I thought the source of this helpful guidance was the Holy Spirit, but as it often felt that it was a group that was helping me, I later described it as angels, guides, or just "the helpers." Once in a while, as I was doing a healing session, this guidance would take the form of someone's deceased mother or father, but I never really gave that much thought.

The relationship I *was* aware of was with a pool of loving, wise guides/healers/teachers that helped me both in my own life's struggles and in the healing, guidance, and teaching that I did to serve others.

It never occurred to me that some of this help I was receiving might be from my own grandparents or other people I knew who had died.

But now, after having had these experiences of my mom showing up, it was time to investigate this whole strata of spirit world communication, what I now know is called "contact with deceased loved ones." In other words, not just guides and angels, but everyday *people* who have died.

Where to go to find out? Lily Dale, of course! Mediumship is the core of the Lily Dale Assembly community. For more than a century, mediums there have been making contact with people who have passed to the world of spirit but still have loved ones here who wish to contact them.

Thus started my education and training in this wonderful world of possibility with spirit people (and animals!) who continue to love us and care about our well-being, even in their now less-physical state.

The teachers of these many classes were extraordinary people (in the truest sense of the word, definitely beyond the ordinary!) with fascinating experiences I had never even thought of. Certainly not what we might normally hear or read about in the media. To them the spirit world was not *out there* or *up there*, but right *here*, right now!

I kept remarking to myself that these very special people had so much to offer the rest of us—to open our perspectives, widen our beliefs, refresh our ideas. However, many of the mediums were not interested in keeping abreast with the new technology and did not have blogs, websites or books. That meant only a few of us got to hear their stories and perspectives.

BING!!

Through a Medium's Eyes Series

About Life, Love, Mediumship and the Spirit World

The light goes off, and an idea is born to create a series of short books that share with the rest of us these mediums' unique and wonderful perspectives of the nonphysical world, as well as how that wider vision has informed their own philosophies, beliefs, and understandings about this world we live in.

And so this series of books was born.

Hopefully you will find them both interesting and expanding of your own world and vision.

Ruth Shilling
August 2016

CHAPTER ONE

Who is

B. Anne Gehman?

Story: Missing Boy

It was the third day of a mediumship class I was attending with the Rev. B. Anne Gehman at the Lily Dale Assembly in New York, USA. Anne had a graceful way of beginning each class on time without it feeling rushed.

She didn't need to raise her voice when it was time to begin because as soon as she stood up in front of the class, everything quieted down immediately. She carried a presence that awed us a bit and elicited both our respect and love.

On this day, however, she arrived just at the last minute before class was scheduled to begin. Her first words were an apology that she wasn't there earlier. Before leaving that morning, the police had telephoned her about a missing boy. Could she locate him?

She searched for him in her special way and found where he was located. She gave that location to the police who promised to call her at noon (when our class broke for lunch) to tell her what they had found. We were all concerned and eager to hear what had happened.

The result? "He was just where I said he would be," she told us later, "and he was still alive." What a relief! And how grateful we all felt that Anne was able to use her special gifts to save this boy.

As I learned more about Anne Gehman, I discovered that this event was a common occurrence in Anne's life. She had telepathically located hundreds of missing persons, many of them children who had been abducted. Her accuracy in locating these children was outstanding, but the events did not always have such a happy ending.

Story: Both Sorrow and Joy

In another case she was asked to locate a missing girl. In her mind's eye* Anne found her, but the girl was no longer alive. What Anne saw was where the girl and her little dog had been buried.

But ... as Anne was looking, she saw there was also a boy in that location, and he was still alive. At that point he had not even been reported missing, but he had been abducted. With the information she gave the police, they were able to find him immediately and save his life.

As Anne remembered this story she sighed. "Little Richard," she said. "I can still see his little face."

During the summer of 2016 I was delighted to do a series of interviews with Rev. Gehman in her attractively decorated home in Lily Dale, NY. Those interviews are the basis of this book.

Anne is poised, gracious and beautiful, and carries an almost queenly air, a demeanor that immediately elicits respect, while at the same time shows a woman who is humble, accessible, easy to talk to, and gently playful.

---

*See more about Remote Viewing on page 62.

Although I know that she has personal relationships with many of the power players of our world—politicians, royalty, media personalities and CEOs—the way she greets me, and all who visit her, is not based on my position in the world. It is *who we are* that matters, and with her psychic perceptions we cannot hide just what that is!

So who is this Rev. B. Anne Gehman? Where did she come from? And how did her life as a medium, healer, counselor, and teacher unfold?

Biographies have already been written about her remarkable life. *There Is A Purpose* is a biography that tells of the earlier chapters in her life and many of the astounding occurrences associated with her.

The Priest and the Medium: The Amazing True Story of Psychic Medium B. Anne Gehman and Her Husband, Former Jesuit Priest Wayne Knoll, PhD by Suzanne Giesemann, tells of their storybook romance, as well as more about the later chapters in her life of eight decades. Dr. Knoll passed to spirit in 2013.

This book, the first volume in the *Through a Medium's Eyes* series, will give the reader a brief overview of her life, but focus mainly on her perspectives—how she sees this earthly life we lead, and also how that relates to the spirit side of life.

A SHORT BIOGRAPHICAL SKETCH
of REV. B. ANNE GEHMAN

Born the eighth and youngest child of a Mennonite family in Michigan, USA, Anne grew up in a quiet, loving and safe environment. Her parents were deeply spiritual, but not dogmatic in their beliefs. As Anne's special gifts became apparent, she was not criticized, made fun of, or told that what she was seeing was wrong.

Anne's Grandmother
Gehman
(her paternal
grandmother)

Anne's grammar school years were in Michigan, but the family later moved to Florida. The schooling in her Mennonite community only went as far as the 8th grade. Most girls married and had children by age 16 or 17, but Anne wanted to continue her education, so when she was 14 she moved away and continued on with a high school education.

To support herself during high school, she worked three jobs. After school she worked at a local nursing home. In the evening she babysat for a single mother until midnight (little did she know at the time that this woman was a prostitute).

From midnight until morning she stayed at the house of an elderly woman who lived alone and needed someone there during the night.

After graduating from high school, Anne went to nursing school. She held a number of jobs in addition to doing mediumship and married for the first time when she was 31. Her daughter from that marriage has now gifted her with four grandchildren, the shining lights in her life.

Oil Painting of Anne by Dolly Anderson Roberts. Her waist-length hair was braided and piled high on her head.

During her career as a medium, healer and teacher, Anne has worked with the police in solving crimes, helped oil companies locate oil, participated in psychic research projects, assisted bereaved family members by connecting with their loved ones, facilitated healings and spiritual growth, been a teacher and inspiration to many student mediums, traveled throughout the world as a medium and counselor to royal families as well as everyday people, assisted government officials in Washington, DC, raised both race horses and appaloosas, founded a Spiritualist church and the Knoll Institute for Spiritual Studies (KISS), served as a registered medium at the Lily Dale Assembly, been featured in the HBO movie *No One Dies in Lily Dale*, and authored a book with Ellen Ratner, *Self-Empowerment—Nine Things the 19th Century Can Teach Us About Living in the 21st*.

Information about Anne Gehman has been included in many books, including *Miracle Workers: America's Psychic Consultants* and *Adventures in the Psychic* both by Jess Stern; *You Can Communicate with the Unseen World Featuring World-Famous Psychic Anne Gehman* by Harold Sherman; and *After Life Experiments: Breakthrough Scientific Evidence of Life After Death* by Gary E. Schwartz, PhD, with William L. Simon.

She has also been written about in magazines, including *Life*, *Time*, and the *Readers' Digest*.

Anne is now a year-round resident at the Lily Dale Assembly where she continues with the spiritual consultations and readings that she began doing at age 15. Those who are lucky enough to get a reading from her during the *Monday Night Circles at Lily Dale* often have no idea just who the gracious, soft spoken person is who sits in front of them.

Anne's website is bannegehman.com.

Anne's House in Lily Dale, NY

USING HER INTUITION

I wondered how having such good intuitive abilities had helped Anne in her everyday life. It was difficult for her to pick out exact instances because she said she is just using it all the time. There isn't any time when she shuts her intuition off. However, she did think of this story to use as an example.

Story: Her Intuition Paid Off

Anne: I read a newspaper ad for "Middle-aged woman experienced in real estate for Cape Coral." I was just 18 or 19 years old and didn't know anything about real estate, but I answered the ad and got the job!

What they wanted was people to telephone and set up bus trips to Cape Coral, which was how they advertised it. We would go into the office every morning, and they would give us a big stack of *lead cards*. I would thumb through them and pick out eight or ten and put the others aside. I would always be able to book those eight or ten for the tour. And then I'd be finished for the day. The others would be working late, but I had more sales than anybody!

SPIRITUAL INFLUENCES

I asked Anne when she first became aware of her spirit guides and teachers. She responded that she had been aware of them for as long as she could remember. The learning for her was to gradually understand that other people could not see or hear what it was that she was aware of.

Story: Foursquare Gospel Church

Anne: When I was 8-12 years old, I used to sneak out on Wednesday nights to go down to the Foursquare Gospel Church to get saved. I'd have my little glass of wine, and I'd go up to the altar.

Brother Smith was a big man with *huge* hands and he would *pounce* his hands down on top of my head in prayer to remove the horrible sins of my life. I thought that was the greatest thing! I loved it because as he did that I'd feel that energy go through my whole body. He was an awesome healer.

After we all went up to get saved at the altar, then people would go forward to be healed. I saw some remarkable things take place there.

I remember one woman fell on the ice as she was coming into the church. Her leg was broken. The bone was sticking right out!

They took her up to the altar, and had her lie down there. Brother Smith put his hands on her and prayed. Oh, my God! He prayed speaking in tongues. I remember seeing that bone go right back into her leg and her leg straighten out.

She walked out of the church that night. I saw some amazing things there with Brother Smith.

I also remember being in that church and going into a trancelike state. I was down on the floor, and I was speaking in tongues, too.

––––––––––

Anne first discovered Spiritualism at age 14 when she met Wilbur Hull, a spiritualist in Cassadaga, Florida. By the age of 15 she was already doing public mediumship in Spiritualist churches and was the youngest person to ever be certified by the NSAC, the National Spiritual Association of Churches.

HEALING

"I just love the healing part of our ministry," Anne said, and then continued to explain that there are different types of healing.

Absent Healing. Sending healing to someone at a distance through positive prayer.

Contact Healing. The healer transfers healing energy to the recipient through touch or moving the hands through the aura of the recipient. The spiritual healer may act as a transformer of the spiritual energy, enabling it to be more readily absorbed by the recipient. Contact with the recipient's hands, shoulders and head is sufficient.

Spirit Healing. Spirit doctors work directly on the recipient without the use of a physical-body healer.

Magnetic Healing, without Spirit Intervention. A person with an abundance of physical life-force magnetic energy helps to transfer this to the recipient. This can deplete the magnetic healer's own energy reserves.

Suggestive Healing. The thoughts of the recipient are influenced through implanted positive suggestions and directions of healing. This can include affirmations.

Self-Healing. This can include prayer, affirmations, or contact with spirit for spirit healing.

Healing Groups. Multiple healers share a common focus of healing for recipients.

HEALING SESSIONS with ANNE

Anne: I begin by having the person sit down in a chair facing me, and I lead them into a meditative state. While they are in that meditative state, I stand behind them and place my hands on them, usually on their shoulders.

Then I am guided by spirit. Often I place my hands on each side of the head (never on the top), then the neck. Sometimes I make a healing pass over them, about six inches out, through their aura–around their head and shoulder area and then down their back. Never in front. Rarely touching them directly, mostly working through the aura. Then sitting facing them, I hold their hands.

People often feel it as heat and vibrations. I open myself to the direction of spirit as to how long my hands stay in one place. I never touch the front of a person. Only the shoulders, hands and head. There are laws . . .

Story: Mobility Returned!

One woman came in with her arm and hand totally paralyzed. She had had a stroke, or something like that. She was able to completely move her arm and her hand after the healing.

Story: *Walking Again*

Another woman had been in an auto accident. Her right leg was totally numb. She had to be carried in. She was able to walk out. Afterwards, she could move her leg and foot and even walked up the steps back out of my office.

Story: *As a Third Grader*

Anne: I was in school in the third grade. I could see my mother in agonizing pain on the floor at home. I didn't ask if I could leave the school, I didn't ask permission, I just left my school and I ran home, which was probably about ¾ of a mile away.

I found my mother as I saw her psychically, and I placed my hands on her and I just prayed to God, talked to God to make her well. She was having a gallbladder attack. My hands absorbed a lot of the poisons. My hands were a dark greenish bile color because I just took on all the poisons. I just sat there with my hands on her for a long time. I just talked to God and the Holy Spirit to make her well.

She began to feel better and sat up for a while. I felt I needed to run my hands under water. We didn't have hot water in our home. I just let the cold water run over my hands. All the darkness and everything left. And then my hands turned very hot and red and I placed my hands on her again, and prayed for her. So that was one of my first healings.

THIS IS MY PATHWAY

Q: *Did you feel CALLED to mediumship or do you feel it is something you chose to do?*

Anne: I never thought I had a choice—in a very positive way. While I have had other education, I just know this is what I am supposed to be doing. It's truly a calling. I was born to do this. I've done it since I was a child. I've always known this is my pathway and I have never questioned it.

SERVING SPIRIT

Q: *What is your desire in serving Spirit?*

Anne: My desire as a medium is to be able to bring to those I serve the evidence of the continuity of life, with messages that can prove that but also inspire them for their own spiritual growth and unfoldment.

In serving those in *spirit*, it is wanting to help them to find, in a satisfactory way, the communication with their loved ones here, so that they can express their love, the guidance that they often bring, and the upliftment that they bring.

♦♦♦♦♦♦♦♦♦♦♦♦♦♦♦♦♦♦♦♦♦♦♦♦♦♦♦♦♦♦♦

CHAPTER TWO

Teachers & Mentors

Anne: My mother and dad were always very supportive of my experiences. I don't think they truly understood everything, or understood mediumship, but they realized that I was a little different and I experienced life differently than a lot of people do. They never criticized. Nobody ever made fun of me. It was just the way it was. They accepted my reality.

They were really my teachers about both spirituality and life. Daddy (born 1886) was always in deep thought, and read the Bible every day. He also read the Torah and Buddhist writings. He loved comparative religion.

My mother (born 1893) was always a prayerful person. My dad was more religious, but I think Mama had a way of sort of accessing more from universal consciousness. She was an amazing person. Joyful and creative, and always a wonderful sense of humor.

Q: *What do you think your mother would like everyone in the world to know?*

Anne: I think my mother would like everyone to know they are a perfect child of God. That they have within them great talent and awareness, and that through prayer, through meditation, through quietness, recognition of God, the spirit world, the angel world, they can access that. They, too, can access those spiritual gifts, whether it is art or music or various forms of mediumship, creativity . . .

Everyone has special talents within them.

Everyone has a certain access to originality.

[In addition to raising her eight children], Mama was a wonderful seamstress. She took in sewing, and worked at a hospital, too. In her early years she was a teacher at a normal school.

Everyday Activities as an Opportunity for Connection

Mama spent so many hours at the sewing machine. That was her time of thinking, accessing that higher consciousness. If she was canning vegetables or fruit, if she was cleaning, whatever she was doing, I remember her always connecting outside of herself.

It's almost as though she used her work as an altar to reach outwardly and upwardly. She saw her responsibilities as a homemaker as a link with God, with Spirit.

Even if she was hanging up clothes on the clothes line, she'd love the sky and the green grass and the birds flying from tree to tree, and the wind that blew the clothing to dry. All of that. There was always a sacredness about it.

Q: *How do you think she kept that focus, to make that connection? Do you know how she did it?*

Anne: I think it was just natural for her, because she had such an open, loving, warm heart. I don't know if she had any specific way of unleashing that. It was more like picking a beautiful flower and seeing the beauty in it, God's love and creation.

She used to say so often, "Flowers are God's smiles to the world."

My Dad left his childhood home at an early age. He sort of rebelled. He was the only one is his family to ever go to college. He had only three years of education (1st - 3rd grade). He was working on a farm for a man who was a professor at Michigan State University. That man recognized my father as a real genius, which he was!

The professor arranged for my dad to be tested and to go to college. Dad graduated from Michigan State University and was written up in the newspaper as "the oldest and wisest graduate!"

He and my mom were always so in love.* They were always so romantic with each other. Always touching and kissing, even when they were old. I never heard an argument or an unkind word. They were always so grateful and kind to one another. There was always such happiness.

WILBUR HULL

Anne met Spiritualist medium Wilbur Hull when she was 14 years old. Wilbur taught her about spiritualist philosophy and shepherded her through the beginnings of her public mediumship.

Anne: One thing I so appreciated in my teenage years was that I had a wonderful mentor with whom I was able to talk about my experiences, and he would share his with me as well. He gave me such a strong understanding of so much about life.

---

*Note: There is more about Anne's parents and photos of them both in this book's final chapter, *Philosophies, Beliefs & the Power of Love.*

Wilbur Hull
Spiritualist
Medium
Cassadaga, Florida

In my mediumship, Wilbur pushed me to get detail. When I would give a message from spirit, he'd say, "Now get all the meat off the bones." He meant by that, get all the detail that you can. When you see a spirit entity, describe them but also go into detail with everything that you see.

Not just, "Your grandmother is here. She's got white hair and blue eyes." You need more than that.

And not just about appearances, but also the content of the messages. So if an entity was giving a message about encouraging someone to go back to school . . . OK, what school, where, what subject matter, what period of time?

Upliftment for All

He also always stressed that a public demonstration of mediumship (in a group setting) should be *uplifting* for everyone present, not just the person receiving the reading. It took me a long time to understand what he meant by that.

When spirit is working, all those who are listening can feel *that flow of energy and love* from the spirit world, so that brings upliftment to them as well.

OTHER TEACHERS

Wilbur Hull was also an excellent trance medium. He would enter a trance state which allowed different spirit entities to speak through him. These spirit teachers helped Anne to develop herself spiritually and philosophically.

Rose was a well known medium who had been Wilbur's teacher. After she passed away, she worked through him (while he was in trance). She was a French Belgian woman with a heavy French accent. Rose would begin with a talk on a certain subject and then answer my questions. She was really a wonderful teacher.

Louise Ward was another teacher who taught me through Wilbur. They both gave me a lot of personal guidance, but it was mostly philosophy.

Q: *What qualities did Wilbur have that you feel are important for a teacher to have?*

Anne: Certainly love, a loving way of pushing, without being demanding or hurtful at all. Sort of a loving push.

Q: *When you are teaching, what qualities do you attempt to embody?*

Anne: Listening. Listening carefully both to the students and to spirit. For example, if a student wants to share something with you, to be a good listener, and get the detail of what they are experiencing. Then listen to spirit to get advice or guidance pertaining to that.

Also, being nonjudgmental, that's a major thing. You don't judge them or judge what they are saying or experiencing. You accept whatever they are sharing with you without judgment.

MENTORING TODAY'S CHILDREN

"All children are psychic. All children have a connection with the spiritual realm," Anne says matter-of-factly. Of course what often happens is parents say things like, 'That's just your imagination," or even laugh at what children say.

Instead, Anne wished to encourage parents to help their children explore their experiences and sort things out for themselves through easy discussions.

The adult can ask, "What else can you tell about that?" or "How did you feel with that?" in such a way that the child knows they can trust the adult to be open-minded and supportive. There can be encouragement to be prayerful to God, to Spirit, in a way that lets the child explore what that is to them, (rather than a story about a big man up in the sky...).

What goes along with this is honoring and listening to the child's own rhythm and timing as to when to address the more profound questions in life.

It's wonderful when kids learn:
- To trust their intuition.
- To be open-minded.
- To know that they are guided with love from the spiritual world, and that in times of fear or concern they can let their mind turn to that source.

Children learn from who their parents are and what they do, more than what they say. Anne's father was a meditator. She remembers watching him, every day at a particular time, sitting in his library chair to meditate and pray. So at a very early age she found her place to sit quietly because she wanted to be like her dad.

See also *Children In The Spirit World*, page 38.

CHAPTER THREE

Guidance & Inspiration

Q: *Where do you turn when you need guidance?*

Anne: I first go into a meditative state, attune myself with that higher source–that Divine Source, or God, and the Holy Spirit. After that I open to my spirit guides and teachers.

I try to do that every day. I just feel and sense. Sometimes I actually hear a voice, but not often. It's more of a telepathic transference.

They very rarely give guidance about anything of a mundane level. It's more the higher teachings, and sometimes philosophical or psychological things.

When I was younger they gave more specific guidance, how to handle situations, things like that.

Example: There was one time where I had quite a disagreement with a friend. They guided me through that to see the way she was thinking, and how I was thinking, and the differences. Not *how* I should think about it, but to give me the perspective. They have done that for me many times.

As I go along through my day, I just know they are involved in my life in a loving, wonderful way.

SPIRIT GUIDES & TEACHERS

Anne explained that there are usually one or two spirit guides that are permanent in our lives, and then there are those that come in and out, usually to help with something in particular or to assist us through a particular period in our lives.

Q: *When were you first aware of the wise and loving guidance from the spirit world?*

Anne: I believe I was always aware of spirit entities. As a very little girl I had what is often called "imaginary playmates," but they were just as real to me as my other friends.

Story: Honto and the Disfigured Arm

I was very aware of a Native American woman named Honto, who was often with me. I didn't realize other people couldn't see her. We used to walk hand in hand.

One day a neighbor asked my mother if there was something wrong with my arm because I was always walking with my arm stuck out to the side. I was just holding Honto's hand!

Q: *Did they help you with things you needed to know or did you just play with them as a kid?*

Anne: I don't know as that there was so much *play* with them as there was being aware of their presence, and their guidance, and their protection.

Story: Helpful Guidance as a Child

As a child I always walked everywhere. We didn't have a car or any other means of transportation. Walking home from school, there were several ways I could go.

One day I wanted to walk home a particular way, but they [the guides] told me not to go that way. Later I learned that a child had been abducted along that pathway.

Q: *So you did what they told you?*
I never questioned spirit at all, and never felt any fear. I always felt such a loving protection from Spirit.

Q: *Are you still in touch with Honto?*
Anne: Oh, yes, definitely.

ANNE'S OTHER GUIDES

My first teacher, Wilbur Hull, was a wonderful trance medium. Through him, Sally spoke directly to me for the first time. It was such a remarkable experience. Sally speaks to others through me now.

There was a Dr. Jackson who came into my life in my teenage years when I began to work with healing. He was also very present when I was in nursing school. And yes, he was someone who had lived on the earth plane.

Anne went on to explain about the different guides who came through to assist with different areas she was involved in. There were the ones who helped when she worked with law enforcement. There were medical guides who helped with healing, and different guides who assisted when she worked with government officials. There was a guide named Red Feather who was especially helpful when she worked for Phillips Petroleum Company and other oil companies to locate oil reserves.

While some of the guides she worked with specialized in particular subjects, others were the ongoing guides who were associated with the particular individuals she was assisting.

Anne emphasizes that we ALL have guides who do their best to assist us throughout our lives. Some probably have a more difficult job than others!

HOW TO BEGIN ACCESSING GUIDANCE

Anne recommends:
1. Reading from various sources
2. A daily practice of meditation and prayer.

1. Reading from various sources (not just one, but many different sources). Fill your mind, heart and soul with information of an inspirational, philosophical and psychological nature. This can become a vocabulary for spirit.

Anne feels that while the sacred writings, such as the Bible or Talmud, still apply to us today, they were written for people in those particular time periods. It is often easier for us to attune to the more contemporary writings.

In Tune with the Infinite by Ralph Waldo Trine is the most wonderful book. Anyone from any religion could read it. It's very universal.

It is uplifting, inspiring and motivating. A beautiful book. When I first got it I couldn't put it down. After that I would go back to it almost every day and read different bits and pieces of it.

2. Establish a daily practice of meditation and prayer. I feel that's essential in our lives.

Prayer (active, asking)

A process of finding an alignment or an attunement with the Divine, and then asking for guidance and assistance in growth and unfoldment.

Meditation (passive, receiving)

Finding that passive state of consciousness, and opening up to receive. Letting the thoughts in your mind go.

Connecting with Guides & Teachers in Spirit

Let your mind be very passive to receive, without making any demands. Sometimes people can become very focused on what or who they want, and they might close out something else even more wonderful.

Often times people may want to communicate with Grandma or Grandpa or their mother, dad, brothers, sisters, and that's fine–nothing wrong with that–but go to a higher source first, and then open to that which is closer to the mundane world.

WAYS to RAISE YOUR VIBRATION

Physically
- Deep/rhythmic breathing, exercise, singing, dancing
- Contact with water (shower, swimming, washing the dishes...)
- Wearing bright and cheerful colors
- Playing with children, cuddling, loving

Mentally
- Concentrate on the positive aspects of your life
- Be thankful for what you have
- Read things that are inspirational, uplifting, comical
- Repeat affirmations, prayers
- Enjoy music, art, nature, flowers, birds, creativity

Spiritually
- Meditate
- Pray to God/Infinite Intelligence
- Surround yourself with white light
- Project healing, loving, pink cloud of light to others
- Call on your spirit guides & teachers to clear your aura
- Visualize the spirit world
- Send crown chakra energy out and up toward your spirit guides

◆◆◆◆◆◆◆◆◆◆◆◆◆◆◆◆◆◆◆◆◆◆◆◆◆◆◆◆

CHAPTER FOUR

The Spirit World

Q: *What is the place the Spiritualists call Summerland?*

Anne: It is simply the spiritual realm. Andrew Jackson Davis and others describe definite layers of seven planes.

I don't think there are definite layers or different planes, because it is all one, but it can help to visualize it as different levels for different vibratory frequencies.

I think it just becomes more and more refined while moving outward and upward.

Those vibratory frequencies, or "levels," also manifest as sound and color. When people sit in circles, I have noticed what level, or how they are connecting, by what colors they see.

Q: *What happens when we die?*

Anne: First of all, it is important to recognize that we are spiritual beings. We have a spirit body and a physical body. What we call death is an illusion. There is no death. There is a continuity of life of the higher mind and the soul.

What happens at what we call death is simply the spiritual body leaving the physical. According to our development—intellectually, spiritually, emotionally—it goes to a different "level."

Those who are totally unevolved and the worst criminals in the world are probably in that lower level where we are told there is darkness. I don't know that as a fact. I would see it, not necessarily as darkness, but as a heaviness and a lack of refinement.

I also believe that we can be in more than one level at a time. If we have really evolved intellectually, that part of us can go to a more refined level. And if we are evolved psychologically or spiritually, I think there is that counterpart.

When I meditate I elevate myself to another level, and those in the spirit world bring themselves downward so we meet.

ANIMALS in the Spirit World

Q: *Do our pets still take an interest in us after they pass over?*

Anne: Absolutely! Absolutely they do! Very often in readings people's pets will manifest. I've seen yappy little dogs and quiet passive ones, and cats, too.

Story: Elizabeth Ann

I was giving a lady a reading and I heard the name "Elizabeth Ann." The woman started to cry. After a few minutes she was able to compose herself, and she said that Elizabeth Ann was her little dog who had just passed away a few days before. That little dog manifested with her name so clearly.

I also remember seeing that the dog was being held by the woman's father (in spirit). He was the one who had brought the dog in.

Story: Spirit Dog at Her Feet

During one entire reading I was aware of a dog (in spirit) sitting at a woman's feet. When I described him, she confirmed how he looked, "and that's exactly where he always sat."

Q: *So do you think our pets sort of stop in to see us?*

Anne: Yes, it is the same as with the people who are in spirit.

Story: Paw Prints

My little Brigit Marie was 18 when she passed away, which is quite old for a little dog. For several years I saw her and felt her presence.

One time, I don't remember how long it was after she ascended into the other realm, but I was lying on my bed which had a satin bedspread.

I felt just a slight jiggle to the bed, and then I saw her little paw marks coming across the bed in that satin. Just little indentations. And then I actually felt her lick my face. There was a little moisture there, and then I felt her wrap herself around my neck like she always did.

Anne's pets. Susie Marie and Wilbur, her kitty friend.

PEOPLE in the Spirit World

Q: *How much are the people in spirit aware of us and our lives? Are they around us 24/7 or . . . ?*

Anne: I think they give us our privacy when that's important to do so. (Laughter)

I think they are around us always at appropriate times to guide us. I don't think they attach to us to be with us *all* the time.

For example, when I feel my husband Wayne's presence, oftentimes it is when I am doing something we would have enjoyed doing together. Like when I sit down for dinner, I feel his presence, whether I am at home or I am out with friends. That's something we really enjoyed together, our meals and our friendship ties.

I often feel him with me when I go to church or if I am out for a walk. He loved the grandkids. I always see him around when the kids are here.

Q: *If we are thinking about our loved ones, does that bring them closer?*

Anne: It can. It depends on what their personality is like.

Q: *Do people's personalities change when they are in the spirit world?*

Anne: Because there is constant evolution, I think that everyone goes through changes. We change from our teenage years to adult life to our old age, and we go through personality changes. I think we do that in the spiritual world as well.

EVOLVING IN THE SPIRIT WORLD

I think the worst criminal can reform in the other world. Part of their growth might be reaching back through the spiritual realm to help others in some way. And that is part of their evolution.

Another example might be someone who was alcoholic* and through their behavior as an alcoholic was abusive to their family or loved ones. I can think of *many* readings where such a person would come through and apologize for their behavior under the influence of alcohol, and then express their regret of how they hurt people.

---

* See page 52 for a story of an alcoholic father.

Sometimes they are very specific about it. Usually they will show me, or I can see and can tell the recipient how that person has changed and how they have evolved.

Story: Where Both Evolve

Not too long ago I was giving a reading for a woman who very much wanted to be a writer. She was a very creative person. She spoke beautifully and eloquently, even just in general conversation.

When I was giving her a reading, her father came through and described how he was helping her with finding that full and free expression with words and with writing. Apparently, he had all of that knowledge and that ability, but he didn't use it while he was here.

So as she is opens to the influence of spirit, and he is able to work through her or influence her, that gives her growth. But because he is helping her, he finds growth. So he was evolving in the other world, by helping her to evolve here.

I think a lot of life is that of service and helping one another. That's really what a lot of it is about.

CHILDREN IN THE SPIRIT WORLD

Anne explained that what people called *imaginary playmates* are often actually young people who passed on at an early age. Those who "die young" continue to grow up in the spirit world and will want to have the experience of playing with other children, just as they would have done if they had continued with the earth life. So those spirit children will often come and play with children here.

There were a number of spirit children who came to play with Anne. There were some Native American children, as well as a girl who had been born in a town near where Anne grew up.

Q: *What do you anticipate happening when you make your own transition into spirit?*

Anne: When I pass to the other world I know I will be reunited with Wayne, all of my siblings, my mother and father, and many from my ancestral past who I know I will recognize although I did not know them here . . . and all of the guides and teachers I have known through this lifetime, such as Honto and Red Feather. I also hope to feel some connection with the great master teachers, such as Jesus and Buddha.

◆◆◆◆◆◆◆◆◆◆◆◆◆◆◆◆◆◆◆◆◆◆◆◆◆◆◆◆◆◆◆

CHAPTER FIVE

Mediumship

ACCESSING THE SPIRIT WORLD

Anne: I believe, always first an attunement with that Divine Source, and secondly with the spirit world.

I never open up to the spirit world first, nor do I advise that to anybody. I think when you feel aligned with that Higher Consciousness, that Infinite Intelligence of the Universe, when you have found that sense of upliftment and attunement on a higher level, *then* you open to spirit.

Never in reverse. One thing I see with some mediums is they want to reach immediately to grandma and grandpa, guides and spirit teachers, and in my opinion, that's the wrong approach. You want first that divine presence, and secondly, the angel world.

Process

1. Relax your body.
2. Let your mind become very passive.
3. Find your attunement with the Infinite.
4. Open yourself to the spirit world.

Q: *Can you, as a medium, always access the people that recipients are wanting to connect with?*

Anne: Not always immediately. I always tell the recipient to let their mind be very clear. Just be open to the inflow of whatever comes. Whoever comes through is what is right this time. I don't like to focus on any particular spirit entity, but *usually* those that they want to hear from will be there. Probably *always* I could almost say.

HINTS for RECEIVING A GOOD READING

Anne gives the following suggestions to those who are going for a reading with a medium.

1. Make sure you go to a medium at a time that you can be very relaxed and open minded.

2. Don't go after a heavy meal.

3. Never use alcohol before going for a reading.

4. It's helpful if you have a need, or prioritize your needs. In your own consciousness be aware that you want to receive from your loved ones. You want to receive some evidence so you know who they are, but don't demand that from the medium.

5. A day or two before the reading, tell your people in spirit that you are going for a reading and make your requests to them. Then let it go.

6. Bring a recording device to the reading and record it. This will enable you to just be present during the reading and not be trying to remember everything. It also means that when you listen to it later, you can pick up evidential details you may have missed while the reading was going on.

Q: *If the recipient is too focused on hearing from someone, can that block it in a way?*

Anne: I think it can.

HOW TO CHOOSE A MEDIUM

The best way to choose the medium who is right for you is your own intuition! Your people in spirit can guide you in a good direction. Just sit quietly and let spirit guide you in that. Be open to their influence.

DURING THE READING: The Role of the Recipient (the person receiving the reading).

1. Remain as open as possible and receptive to whatever comes through. Being passive and prayerful is the best mode to be in.

2. Do not have a demanding attitude. If you already have an idea what you want to hear, that really gets in the way.

3. Do not have a strong focus on someone in your mind. Do not think strongly of people's names or how they look. If you do, the medium may pick that up through thought transference instead of making an authentic connection to them in spirit.

4. You should not need to tell the medium anything but you also don't want to be totally closed. Wait and be receptive to what they bring forth. You can confirm what they are saying, but let them tell you the information.

Anne: You want to be open, but a medium doesn't need to know anything about you. I ask a person's first name, maybe where they're from, and a birthday (which I use for doing prophecy).

5. Wait until afterwards to evaluate. Record the reading. Evaluating while you are in the reading puts you into the wrong mode (left brain interference). Making a recording enables you to save the evaluating for when you listen later.

Anne: First of all, when a person comes for a reading, I don't like them to demand answers or communication with any particular spirit, but just to be open and let it flow through.

There is something wonderful when you can just open your mind and feel God's love and that presence of the Spirit, that collective spirit, the Holy Spirit, and just let that flow through you and around you. There's just something so beautiful about that.

And then, as a medium, you can tap into that Spirit in different places and receive the identity of those loved ones. But when a person comes and someone close to them has just passed away and they are hoping to have contact with them, I am open to that, too. I pray for them, I would be prayerful about it, then I would guide them to just be open and receptive to whatever comes.

Story: What was the Cause?

There was a woman here recently whose daughter had passed away. She knew her daughter had been taking drugs and alcohol, but she wasn't sure what it was that took her life.

When I made contact with the girl, I felt like there were blood vessels bursting in her head. It was brought on by the drugs and alcohol, but they were not the actual cause at the end.

This information was what the mother wanted to know. And it turned out that it also matched the results of the autopsy.

THE COMMUNICATORS IN SPIRIT

They already know what the need is.

Anne: A lot of times when somebody dies in an accident, the person receiving the reading is eager to know *how* that happened—were there drugs, alcohol, was there somebody else who caused it, did their person cause it . . .

That information usually comes through first. The person in spirit is usually very eager to bring that information, to bring clarification about it.

I would rather the person not ask that, but just be open to receive, because *usually* the communicating spirit will know what that person wants. They already know what the need is, so they will bring that forth.

Q: *Do the people in spirit know what we are thinking?*

Anne: They are very much aware of what we are thinking. There is a telepathic communication that goes on all the time.

Q: *Why is it that some people in spirit come through so much more often than others. For example someone might find that their grandmother always comes through but not their grandfather?*

Anne: Spirit communication is dependent upon the Law of Attraction and the Law of Love.

She pointed out it could be any of the following:

1. There could be more of a "likeness of consciousness" or vibration between the recipient and the grandmother. Perhaps they were not so close with the grandfather.

2. The medium may resonate with the grandmother more than the grandfather in spirit.

3. The person's grandmother may just be a better communicator than the grandfather.

Q: *What do mediums mean when they say a spirit entity is a good communicator?*

Anne: A good communicator, or an effective communicator, is one who would have a stronger ability to make themselves understood. It helps if there is a lot of love there or a strong desire to communicate and be understood.

If someone was involved in spirit communication during their physical life here or was more aware of the spiritual realms before their passing, they will also find it easier to communicate from the other side.

THE DESIRES OF THOSE IN SPIRIT

Q: *What do the deceased loved ones need or want?*

Anne: They need for us to be open and nonjudgmental, open to their presence.

To feel their love, and know that they can continue to communicate telepathically and lovingly.

There is no real separation between the two worlds except that of our own thinking.

EVIDENCE from the Spirit World

There is always an effort on the part of the communicating spirit to give proof of their identity. They usually will describe themselves, the relationship, maybe something special, a memory that no one else would know–things that would give proof of their identity.

They will also talk about recognizing what their loved one is doing, because the communicating spirit wants their loved ones to know they're there and sees what their life is. They are still there enjoying the companionship of their loved ones.

Stories: Husbands Bring Evidence to Their Wives Showing Their Awareness

A woman, whose husband had passed on recently, was here for a reading the other day. She had just sold her house, and the first thing her husband (in spirit) said when he came through was, "I am so glad that you were able to sell the house, as we had already planned to do."

They had planned to sell their house and they were going to create a new life in their retirement, but he passed away before they had a chance to do so. So he saw that she had done that, and he was pleased with the way she handled it and all that happened. In fact, he even gave some names and some monetary amounts as well.

In another reading a husband (in spirit) came through and talked about a new dress his wife had bought. He gave the color of it, the new shoes she bought . . . also that she had cleaned out the closet and exactly where all his clothes went, and how pleased he was about how she handled all that.

HEALING and MOVING FORWARD

They want to discourage the person from grieving. That is one of the main purposes of the contact. They would like to see that the person on earth is healing and moving on with their life in an appropriate way, without a lot of grief and sorrow.

Not forgetting that person who has crossed over, but not focusing on the sorrow and the pain of that loss.

THE COMPANIONSHIP CONTINUES

It's like any other relationship. If a person moves away somewhere, you want that communication still, to know that they're all right, and that their life is moving on in a new way. When we travel to another country, what is the first thing we want to do? We want to reach back to our homes, our families with a card, a letter, a phone call, to let them know how we are, what we are experiencing.

I think it is the same thing when we travel on to the other world. They want to give evidence to validate that they are really there. For people here to know that they are not really gone, they are just in a different way of being, but they are still with us.

Q: *So you feel that those in spirit want that communication, too, not just us here?*

Anne: Oh, absolutely.

Q: *How would we do that?*

Anne: For the person on earth to open their mind and heart to know when the departed person is with them, and again, that there is that love.

Q: *Do they like it when people go to their grave?*

Anne: No, I think they would rather have the person be prayerful and meditate and feel their presence. They are not anywhere near their grave.

I just don't see that as anything that is particularly helpful, except when the person who is on the earth plane does not have the knowledge and awareness that their loved one is still with them.

Q: *What about when people go and put flowers on a grave or something like that?*

Anne: I think those in spirit like to acknowledge that as a form of love, but wouldn't it be better to just have a bouquet of flowers in memory of the person in your home?

GIVING LOVE & ASSISTANCE

Q: *Do people in spirit have concerns about the people here?*

Anne: I think they always do, and they want to be with their loved ones to assist them. They would not make decisions for us, but they would help us to see things more clearly, often from a broader perspective. Of course, it depends upon their own level of personal development.

My husband, Wayne, was very spiritual, always seeking greater growth–both intellectually and spiritually–so he would be with me to assist me in my process with that.

Q: *Do those in spirit take an interest in the mundane things in our lives?*

Anne: Many times when spirit speaks of the mundane things, it is more an effort to have the individual know that they are aware of what's going on in their lives, and that they want to help and support them.

Those in spirit have usually grown beyond the focus on the mundane things and are more interested in the person's spiritual or psychological growth and unfoldment.

However, we cannot totally separate the spiritual and the material. We can't totally separate that because this material world is a vehicle of the spirit at this time. And many times the material concerns we have are also part of our spiritual growth and unfoldment.

How we handle the material world and our responsibility–whether it's money or possessions–isn't just materialistic. It's moral, it's ecological, so we can't totally separate the two.

WHEN THERE IS DISCORD

Anne: If there was wrongdoing by the person in spirit, he will be very eager to see those he hurt find their healing.

Q: *What about if there is discord with two people and one has crossed over. Do you think a medium can help with healing that?*

Anne: I think a medium can help with that, but it's still dependent upon the two people wanting the healing between the two of them to happen.

Story: An Alcoholic Father in Spirit

Anne: I have a client who has been coming to me for years. Her father was alcoholic and sexually abused her as a child and into her teenage years.

I have seen how her healing has taken place by her communication with him, knowing that he could apologize and know that that was wrong, and knowing he is growing in the other world.

Q: *Was there anything he could do to rectify that in any way or did he just have to hope she would be willing to take his apology?*

Anne: Only the apology. But she went to counseling, and she could actually feel his presence in her counseling sessions, so she knew they were both healing.

SUICIDES

Q: *What is your experience with people who have taken their own lives, suicides?*

Anne: What I have found is they're usually very sorry for their behavior and what they did. Often times they'll be more concerned for the fact that they hurt other people in their decision to do that.

They are always regretful about that. That's what I have found.

They see it as sort of selfish, or self-centered, that before doing that they couldn't be considerate of how they were affecting others.

Often times there is a desire on their part to know that those they left behind are finding forgiveness and understanding for why they did that.

Story: An Artist in the Spirit World

I have a client whose son committed suicide. After ten years she is still suffering with this. And while she understands his thinking of why he did this, she hasn't been able to really forgive him because he hurt the whole family so deeply.

And so she struggles with that, and thinks he was very selfish.

He has said that he really regretted his behavior. Not for himself so much, but because he sees how it affected her and others in the family.

He wants them to go on with their lives the way he has done. He has talked about his reunion with many loved ones and relatives in the spirit world. How they have helped him. And he has talked about his work in the spirit world.

He was an artist and a very creative person, and he now (in the spirit world) continues with his artwork, but he also has become knowledgeable in sound and music. He uses that all together—all those vibratory frequencies flowing together. I have learned from him!

He has also talked about a teenager in that family who is very artistic and how he is often *with* that person to inspire and to guide them.

The woman told me later that the teenager feels that presence and feels inspired by him.

Q: *Have you seen times when a contact with someone in the spirit world has resulted in a healing for the recipient?*

Anne: I see that every day! I think anyone who has lost a loved one and has contact with that one in the spirit world, it is very healing. I know that with my husband, Wayne, I feel a lot of healing when I feel his presence and I know that he is well, and good in the other world. And I know that he has found his healing there and no longer has pain.

ADVICE FOR DEVELOPING MEDIUMS

Q. *What's most important for a medium?*

Anne: Always first make an attunement with that Divine Source, and *secondly* with the spirit world.

Q: *What is the first piece of advice you would give to someone beginning to develop their mediumship?*

1. A Daily Practice. See page 27-28.

2. Your own Auric Emanation will Attract.
It's important to realize that every thought, every action, every deed, creates your own personal auric emanation and what you will attract from the spirit world.

So I don't think a person can hang out at bars and attract the best from the spiritual realm. I think if you live a life filled with love and light and positive thinking, that is what you attract into your life.

3. Choose Specific Times for Connecting with Spirit.
I think it is important to have specific times for spirit communication, not to be open to the spirit communication all the time. There are times to be just be here, because we really live in two worlds. You want to *choose* which one you want to be in. Take charge.

DEVELOPMENT CIRCLES

Q: *How important is it for a developing medium to participate in an ongoing development circle?*

Anne: The daily meditations are vitally important. The circle, however, gives people the opportunity to give out their impressions and for spirit to work through them in that particular way and depth. You also have that exchange of energy with others in the group, and visitations with a greater *variety* of spirit entities (more than a person would have sitting alone).

What is it you are bringing to the circle?

Something that is often overlooked today is how you *prepare* for the development circle. For example, we would not eat a heavy meal, we would never have anything alcoholic, we would drink a lot of water. We would have meditation *prior to going* to a circle.

That way we were taking into the circle that sense of upliftment and love and joy.

DEVELOPMENT CIRCLE COMPONENTS

1. Prayer and Meditation

It is always appropriate to start with prayer and meditation, of course, so that people enter that very relaxed, spiritual state of consciousness.

2. A Time of Silence

There should always be a time of silence. It is in the

silence that spirit is working with you, so silence for a period of time is vitally important. If people start speaking right away, that doesn't give spirit any time to really prepare your mind and make that connection between the two worlds *on a deep level.*

You want to have that *time* for spirit to work through you and with you to prepare your mind and body to receive all that connection with the unseen.

FELLOW MEDIUMS and STUDENTS

We want to always bring encouragement and support to our fellow mediums and fellow students. We all can be a wonderful resource for each other.

PUBLIC DEMONSTRATIONS of MEDIUMSHIP

When spirit is working, all those who are listening can feel that flow of energy and love from the spirit world, so that brings upliftment to them as well. So it should be uplifting for *everyone* there, not just those who receive messages.

PRIVATE READINGS & CONSULTATIONS

Q: *What happens in your private consultations?*

Anne: I'm used to seeing people by appointment, sitting down with them, having a few minutes of prayer and meditation together, and then opening to spirit.

I am very grateful for having worked in a dental office. That gave me the professional ethics that I needed. I applied that to my mediumship practice–making appointments, receiving my fee.

SELF-CARE for MEDIUMS

Q: *What about self-care for mediums?*

• A regular meditation practice. Meditation, prayer and keeping attuned to that spiritual consciousness.

• Always seeking new growth and understanding, to continue to read and think and discuss things. To grow not only spiritually, but intellectually and psychologically.

• Deal with your own conditions in life. We all have challenges and difficulties. Deal with those on a daily basis so they don't accumulate.

• Constantly refining your mind and soul.

• Cleanliness–body, mind and spirit.

• Proper diet, proper eating. Eating fresh fruit and vegetables because they carry that live energy.

• Avoiding things that are addictive, like alcohol, drugs, nicotine. I think having a little bit of alcohol occasionally is okay but to avoid it on a regular basis.

◆◆◆◆◆◆◆◆◆◆◆◆◆◆◆◆◆◆◆◆◆◆◆◆◆◆◆◆◆◆

CHAPTER SIX

Psychometry, Apports, Table Tipping, & Remote Viewing

PSYCHOMETRY

Anne: The word *psychometry* comes from two Greek words. *Psycho* meaning *mind* or *soul*, and *metro* or *metron*, to measure. So it is *soul-measuring*, or reading from the soul of things. (In psychology *psycho* has a different meaning.)

An object carries the aura of the person who wore it or who owned it. You can tap into that auric emanation. The aura carries historical events, emotions, locations . . . all of those things are recorded in the aura of the object.

I believe that everyone can be successful with psychometry. When we do it in the classes, people are so amazed at their own ability–to just hold something and be able to see the past or the present and the people connected with that.

Q: *If someone wanted to try psychometry, and they had never done it before, what would they do?*

Anne: They would hold an object that they know nothing about–its history or the people connected with it–but they have to have access to someone who does. Otherwise they wouldn't be able to confirm anything.

Steps for Doing Psychometry

1. Begin by quieting yourself. Quiet your body and mind.

2. If you are right-handed, put the object in your left hand.

3. With your right hand run your fingers over it. As you touch it, you tap into the history of it. Don't think of anything (don't think questions), just go blank and let the object speak to you.

As you touch it with your fingertips, you are feeling the physical aspect of it, but because you are also spirit, your spiritual counterpart is touching into the spiritual counterpart of the object. That then begins to bring pictures, colors, location, heat, cold, emotions . . .

The spiritual counterpart contains all the information about the object.

4. Report whatever it is that you sense and feel, whatever you experience with that.

Another way is to hold the object to your forehead or solar plexus.

PSYCHOMETRY STORIES

Story: The Lost Dog

I remember a woman whose dog had gotten loose and was lost. She brought a collar and a leash to me. She had bought a new one about a week before, but she kept the old one, so she brought that one along. I was able to tap into that and tell her exactly where the dog was.

So she went immediately and found her little dog, then called to tell me.

Story: The Bloody Knife

A friend was here visiting me the other day and he reminded me that when he last visited, we were interrupted by a policeman who came in with a bloody knife in his hand.

The blood was still wet! He handed it to me and wanted a reading on what had happened.

Q: *Were you able to tell him?*
Yes. And they went out and arrested someone.

REMOTE VIEWING

Q: *When you are asked to find something or someone, how are you doing that? How does that happen for you?*

Anne: I see a mental picture, like a vision. I just think of the question (example: Where is so-and-so?). I see pictures and then I draw that. It's just shown to me.

People lose all sorts of things. Lost people, lost things, lost wedding bands, lost dogs, cats, kids, husbands . . .

Q: *Is the information always available, or not?*
Anne: Yes, it is, though sometimes it is more complete and more succinct.

Q: *So you can pretty much always find it?*

Anne: Usually, yes. Sometimes what they are looking for is not in a place they have access to.

I often use an object, like a piece of clothing, and I use that for psychometry. That can help make the contact.

If it is something like a ring that is missing, I ask when they saw it last, the history of the ring or maybe the meaning of it. That can help with tapping into it, too.

Anne also explained that to help someone in finding something, one also needs to include <u>time</u>. What time will so-and-so be in such-and-such a place? As you will see in the following story, it was imperative to know WHEN the person would be in a particular place.

Story: The Cheating Husband

A woman came to me and brought her husband's watch. She knew he was having affairs, so she wanted descriptions and names. Whatever I could tell her.

Q: *Did you do that?*
Anne: Well, I was hesitant, but I thought, "Why not do that, rather than have her spend all that money on a private eye?" So, yes, I did.

I said, "Go to such-and-such a place. Such-and-such a time. Just have the private eye or you be there, you'll see him."

She caught him. It was a hotel and he arrived with a woman. Her attorney sent so many people to me after that!

For more **Remote Viewing Stories** see pages 1-3.

APPORTS: DE-MATERIALIZATION/ RE-MATERIALIZATION

Anne: An *apport* has to do with the passage of matter through space. Spirit is able to dematerialize an object in one location, carry it through space, and re-materialize it in another location.

Story: A Young Man's Coins
This happened with a woman from Washington whose son had died. He collected pennies. There were some other coins, too, but mostly pennies.

The morning of her appointment, one or two of the coins fell on me as I sat in my chair for my morning meditation. When she arrived we went downstairs to my office. All over the steps there were pennies. It was so remarkable.

There must have been more than 40-50 of them, all over the steps. I knew they hadn't been there before, and the woman did not tell me anything. There were also pennies that dropped around us just as we started the reading.

Her son came through right away. I don't remember the content of the reading, but I know that she had a son who had just recently crossed over, in sort of a tragic way, I think. I don't remember the details of that.

I also knew the pennies were his, that he had had a jar of pennies. Anyway, when she got home that day, the pennies from his jar were missing. So we knew they were his.

Story: The Rose

When I lived in Florida I had a rose garden. I just loved my roses. I worked with them every day. A client brought me a new rose bush, knowing that I had the rose garden.

I planted the rose bush. I just loved it. I gave it love and food and water and all. I was very attentive to that particular rose bush. A bud came out and I was watching it carefully every day. I just couldn't wait for it to bloom.

One day, right after my sister passed away, I was so depressed and sad. I went into my living room. I sat down. I remember putting my head back and just resting in the chair.

All of a sudden, I saw these little specks of green coming through the ether, and then little specks of rose color coming toward me. It suddenly took shape, and it dropped right in front of me. Right at my feet.

It was a rose bud. I remember picking it up. I was so amazed. I knew that this was the rose bud from my rose bush. The interesting thing was the stem wasn't cut. It was as if it was sort of *pinched*. There was no real opening on the end of it. It was sort of like a sharpened pencil. Almost like it was plastic and was pulled apart.

As I held it, I went out to the rose bush, and the other end of the stem that it came from was like that, too. It was like it was pinched off. The outer portion of the stem was very tight all around it with no real opening.

I put it in water, and it opened up beautifully. It remained fresh and beautiful for probably a month. It was *beautiful*. Afterwards I pressed it in my Bible. I still have it.

Story: Table Tipping

Ruth: In Anne's weeklong classes she saves Friday for some of the physical phenomena. One Friday we all bent spoons; another Friday we did table tipping.

I had come across a few references to table tipping in books (the Romantic era composer Robert Schumann was said to do table tipping in the 1800's), and I had heard one person talk about doing it with one of the Lily Dale mediums, but I could not imagine it could really happen the way my friend told the story about it.

My understanding was that people sat around in a darkened room with their hands touching a table and asking questions hoping that the table would lurch a bit, bumping a yes or no answer to the questions. One for *yes*, two for *no*, something like that. It seemed like something someone could fake.

It was a sunny day on the Friday that we were to do the table tipping in Anne's class, so we were in broad daylight. No drawing of curtains or anything like that. We were divided into small groups, of four or five, each with a round table in the center.

Other groups seemed to be getting some results, but my group was not having any luck. Maybe it was my skepticism that was bogging things down.

Anne was overseeing everything and came over to our table. She had a light, playful feeling to her. "Oh, dear," she said, "let's see what we can do here."

She leaned over and placed her hands lightly on the table. Ba-bump! Ba-bump-bump-bump! The table was bumping and turning. Anne withdrew and we continued without her as the table began going wild!

We were literally chasing it around as it turned and shot sideways, went up on two legs, and then three legs in the air. It seemed to want to lift right off the floor!

There was great hilarity and laughter as we all spun around with our tables. All of them were doing it!

When things settled and quieted down, Anne encouraged us to feel under the tables for the coolness that was there. It was sort of like sticking your hand into a refrigerator.

Anne seemed a bit disappointed that none of the tables levitated completely that day (ours *almost* did). Evidently they often went completely up into the air, but I was ecstatic! What an amazing experience, and certainly not faked!

ANNE EXPLAINS ABOUT TABLE TIPPING (or TABLE TILTING)

Q: *What is table tipping and how does it work?*

Anne: There are two types of table tipping. You can ask yes and no questions for either type.

1. It can be the energy that is directed by all of the people in the circle, so it's an electromagnetic energy that is not necessarily from spirit. Our minds can direct those answers that are yes and no.

2. It can be spirit *combined* with the energy of the sitters. You can know if it's from spirit because you'll feel the presence of spirit and you'll feel a cool breeze, usually around the feet and under the tabletop.

If the sitters are quite sensitive, they can actually see what is called a *psychic rod*. It's a rod of electromagnetic energy under the table that spirit uses to manipulate the table. As you work with the table tipping, you can actually see and feel the psychic rod (of course not everybody can, but if you are sensitive you can).

Q: *What does the psychic rod look like?*
Anne: It is like a narrow cylinder, a rod of light, about an inch in diameter or less, coming from the floor and up under the table.

Q: *Is it a particular spirit entity that moves the table? Would it be a loved one doing it?*

Anne: It's a collection of energies–electromagnetic energies and spiritual energies, etheric energies–drawn from the sitters and from spirit, but usually people will feel certain entities, people they know in spirit–family members, guides, teachers–they will feel that presence.

Q: *What kind of a state do the sitters need to be in for that to happen?*

Anne: The body needs to be relaxed, and the mind passive and very focused. So the energy becomes focused and the mind will connect that energy with the spirit entities who are communicating.

Q: *What kind of a focus should the sitters have?*

Anne: First to focus on the alignment or attunement with God and secondly with the spirit world. The intent has already been set that the table will move, so all of the focus is up into the spirit world (*not thinking "I hope it moves . . ."*).

SPEAKING IN OTHER LANGUAGES

Story: A Reading in Greek

In Florida I lived not too far from Tarpon Springs, which had a large Greek community. I had a lot of clients that came to Cassadaga to see me from there.

One day a Greek woman called me. She spoke English very well, and said, "My cousin is coming to visit and she does not speak English, so I want to come with her and to interpret your reading."

I agreed that they could sit together, so they came and the woman interpreted for her cousin.

Quite frankly, I was getting a bit impatient (because I had to wait for her to interpret everything I said), when I found that I was speaking in Greek. I was speaking directly to the woman in her own language. That went on for the rest of the hour.

Usually speaking another language is not that unusual when you're in a trance state, but I was not in trance. I was fully aware that I was speaking to her in her language. I had a knowingness of what I was saying, but didn't know any of the words. To my knowledge, I had never been exposed to the Greek language.

Q: *Do you think because you were tuned in to her (the recipient) you picked that up from her energy?*

Anne: I think it was her energy but also the communicating spirit. I think it was both.

Story: Speaking a Tribal Language

Anne: We were visiting a tribe in Brazil. They didn't speak English at all, but we had an interpreter. I found myself again becoming rather impatient with waiting for the interpretation. Suddenly, I found myself starting to talk with the chief of the tribe in his language.

I had a knowingness of what I was saying, but I had never heard that language before either. The interpreter thought I had lied to him about not knowing the language!

UNINVITED SPIRIT CONTACTS

Q: *What is your advice to people who have uninvited contact with people in spirit and don't know how to handle it or control it?*

Anne: I have never had that happen. I might sometimes feel a presence and ignore it, but I just feel they are always all around.

◆◆◆◆◆◆◆◆◆◆◆◆◆◆◆◆◆◆◆◆◆◆◆◆◆◆◆◆◆◆◆◆◆◆◆

CHAPTER SEVEN

Beliefs, Philosophies and the Power of Love

BELIEFS

Anne: I believe in the Infinite Intelligence of the Universe and natural law, the way that nature always does things without change. It is always consistent.

I believe in the brotherhood, the sisterhood, of all humanity. We are all brothers and sisters, regardless of race or creed, position in life, or whatever else.

Q: *Do you believe in God?*

Anne: I don't believe there is *a* God out there, but there is that spiritual counterpart of all that is, that I would call the Infinite Intelligence of the Universe. It is infinite and an expression through all of nature. It's impersonal and ever present.

It's impersonal, but it becomes personal as you feel your attunement with that source. I believe that through prayer and meditation, as you feel the sense of oneness with that source, that's what I would call God. Not *a* God, but God Consciousness.

Q: *Does God, the Infinite Intelligence, have an agenda? Does God have a plan?*

Anne: Evolution. Continuous growth, continuous evolution of mind and soul. And also *refinement* within the physical material world.

We're aware of the evolutionary processes of the universe. That is God Consciousness *evolving* through matter, whether it is plants, animals, whatever.

There is constant change. We may not observe it (it can be slow), but it is happening.

THE GOLDEN RULE

Anne: The Golden Rule is something which has been taught by all cultures, and all different world religions. I think it is the highest principle to live by.

I feel like I want to live every day according to the highest and the best that I know. And I would never want to knowingly hurt anyone at all or take from anyone. And I really believe it is more wonderful to give than to receive, although I like to receive, too! (Laughter)

Q: *What is it that throws people off their path in life and are there ways that can be avoided?*

Anne: I think one thing that throws people off is greed and buying into a materialist pathway. Or sometimes it can be with taking things that alter the consciousness–drugs, alcohol.

Greed places a greater significance on money or material things, as opposed to feeling the strong and beautiful loving connection with God, with Spirit.

We can enjoy things of the material world, but not feel the need, in a greedy way, to hold onto them.

SALVATION

Q: *How have your beliefs changed over time?*

Anne: As a child I believed in the need for a savior God. I believed in the Christian concept of salvation through sacrifice, that we needed Jesus to save us from our sins. I really believed that and I prayed to Jesus as a little girl. I outgrew that in my early teenage years when I began to question a lot of things.

I learned about personal responsibility, that I had to be responsible for my own wrongdoings. No one could take away my own personal responsibility. I then began to see Jesus as the great healer, the great medium, the great teacher.

I now think the higher teachings are a source of salvation because we are saved from wrong thinking and wrong doing.

LOVE

Anne: Love is connected to learning to be nonjudgmental. When we truly love we are forgiving; we accept the flow of things; we're harmonious with our surroundings with a sense of peace; we're not wanting to change anything.

When you have love you also have joy, peace, and creativity. All those qualities are connected with love.

Q: *If you could communicate something to everyone in the world what would you want them to know and understand?*

Anne: I think the most important thing is learning to be nonjudgmental and to love. Many people tend to love conditionally. I think learning unconditional love, which is open-mindedness, being able to harmoniously feel the connection with all things and all people with no judgment, that's what I see as most important.

The most important way to communicate that love and nonjudgment is to demonstrate it in your own life. You can't lecture to people.

Q: *Can you think of anyone who exemplified that to you or does exemplify that?*

Anne: I think my mother and father did. So beautifully. I never heard an unkind word. I never heard a word of judgment, a word of gossip. Everything was so loving and joyful. And we didn't have much. We had very modest means, but everything was always okay.

[Note: Anne was the youngest of eight children in a Mennonite family living in Michigan, USA. They did not have a car or electricity in the house.]

LIVING IN LOVE

My mom and dad were so in love. I never heard them argue. I heard them disagree a few times, but there was never any dispute. It was always loving.

Q: *How was it possible for them to live like that? A lot of people would like to have that but don't. What enabled that to happen?*

Anne: I would say their belief system. They were very spiritual. They weren't filled with dogmas or creeds at all, but they were very spiritual and *they lived it*. They lived what they believed.

They believed in God. They believed in the spirit world. They believed in the guardianship from the unseen world. They believed in prayer and meditation, and allowing that healing and love energy to flow through them and to others out into the world. They believed in being creative–they were both very creative people. They believed in goodness, that it was a good world.

They always saw good in people and in every situation. If there was something a bit negative, they would talk about it and see the higher side of it.

They looked for the good in everything, expecting that it would be there.

Anne's Parents

Johannes Gehman & Beatrice Elizabeth Reigle Gehman

Story: During World War II

My parents were pacifists. They didn't believe in war at all. We had a little radio out in the wood shed (we wouldn't have that in the house, of course). They'd go out and listen to Gabriel Heatter, who was a news commentator–very dramatic–and they would discuss it.

I heard them discussing Hitler one time and how it was important for people to stand up against that evil. They were talking about the good and evil of war. My dad read from the Bible to all of us that night. My dad thought there would be a better way to handle things than going to war and killing people.

Johnny, my eldest brother went into the army. I remember my parents saying, "Well, it's his pathway. God has a pathway for each one of us, and that's his pathway." That's how they accepted it.

My brother disappeared for a while in the war. Three representatives from the army came to the house. They told my mother and dad that my brother had been killed in action.

When they left, my mother sat down and said, "No. They're wrong. He's still alive." She knew he was still alive. I can still feel the emotion of that.

My dad trusted my mother's intuition so much that he agreed with her.

I was just a little tot, but I remember when Johnny came walking up the road to our house. He was home! What a thrill that was.

This popular song was written by Anne's mother, Beatrice Elizabeth Reigle Gehman.

◆◆◆◆◆◆◆◆◆◆◆◆◆◆◆◆◆◆◆◆◆◆◆◆◆◆◆◆

❦❦❦❦❦❦

When It's Over Over There
by Beatrice Gehman

When the trump of marching feet
are heard no more
And the peoples of the earth
are through with war
Then there'll come a dawn,
we'll go marching on
to a new and better land than before.

❦❦❦❦❦❦

List of Stories

Missing Boy   1

Both Sorrow and Joy   3

Her Intuition Paid Off   8

Foursquare Gospel Church   9

Mobility Returned!   12

Walking Again   13

As a Third Grader   13

Honto and the Disfigured Arm   25

Helpful Guidance as a Child   25

Elizabeth Ann   33

A Dog at Her Feet   33

Paw Prints   34

Where Both Evolve   37

What Was the Cause?   44

Husbands Bring Evidence to Their Wives   47
Showing Their Awareness

An Alcoholic Father in Spirit   52

An Artist in the Spirit World   53

The Lost Dog   61

The Bloody Knife   62

The Cheating Husband   63

A Young Man's Coins   64

The Rose   65

Table Tipping   67

A Reading in Greek   70

Speaking a Tribal Language   72

During World War II   79

Anne's Recommended Reading List

In Tune with the Infinite
Author: Ralph Waldo Trine
This is the most wonderful book. Anyone from any religion could read it, as it's very universal. It is uplifting, inspiring and motivating, a beautiful book. When I first got it I couldn't put it down. After that I would go back to it almost every day and read different bits and pieces of it.

- **Our Unseen Guest**
- **The Unobstructed Universe**
- **The Betty Book**
- **The Road I Know**
- **Across the Unknown**

Author: Stewart Edward White
These books are an excellent source for learning about spiritual philosophy and unfoldment. It is best to read these books in the order listed above.

The Teachings of Silver Birch
Author: A.W. Austen
All of the books by Silver Birch are excellent reading, although I don't have the belief that these are a reincarnation.

• **The Rock of Truth or**
Spiritualism, the Coming World Religion
• **The Unfolding Universe**
Author: Arthur Findlay
Arthur Findlay wrote 36 volumes and they are very wonderful books. These books are especially good for people who grew up in an orthodox teaching because it takes that away but then it gives you a replacement for it.

• **On the Edge of the Etheric:**
Survival After Death Scientifically Explained
Author: Arthur Findlay
An excellent book that opens the mind to an awareness of the other world, the spiritual realm.

• **The Curse of Ignorance,** multiple volumes
Author: Arthur Findlay
These are highly recommended for the serious student. They are more like text books.

Books by or about B. Anne Gehman

• **Self-Empowerment:**
Nine Things the 19th Century Can Teach Us
About Living in the 21st
Authors: B. Anne Gehman and Ellen Ratner

• **The Priest and the Medium:**
The Amazing True Story of Psychic Medium
B. Anne Gehman and Her Husband, Former
Jesuit Priest Wayne Knoll, Ph.D
Author: Suzanne Giesemann.
From the book's description, "*The Priest and the Medium* shares the remarkable story of two soul mates on parallel paths with divergent beliefs, yet united in their love for God and each other."

• **There Is A Purpose: The Story of Anne**
Gehman, Psychic Spiritualist
Authors: Jerry McCarty and Debra Quarles
An unauthorized biography of B. Anne Gehman. This book is about the earlier chapters of her life.

• **You Can Communicate with the Unseen**
World: Featuring World-Famous Psychic
Anne Gehman
Author: Harold Sherman

• **Miracle Workers: America's Psychic**
Consultants Adventures in the Psychic
Author: Jess Stern

• **After Life Experiments: Breakthrough**
Scientific Evidence of Life After Death
Authors: Gary Schwartz, PhD, with William Simon

Additional Resources
from Ruth Shilling

Lily Dale Assembly
Lily Dale, NY 14752 USA
(716) 595-8721
www.lilydaleassembly.com
The world's largest center for the science, philosophy and religion of Spiritualism. Classes and activities are mostly offered during the summer months. There are 50+ registered mediums who live and serve there in the daily services.

Arthur Findlay College
Stansted Hall, Stansted, UK
01279 81 3636, 00 44 127 981 3636
www.arthurfindlaycollege.org
A residential facility where students study spiritual and psychic enfoldment, Spiritualist philosophy, Spiritualist healing, and kindred disciplines. Considered to be the foremost school for Evidential Mediumship in the world.

The Journey Within Church

25 Carr St., Pompton Lakes, NJ 07442 USA

(973) 616-9685

www.journeywithin.org

The pastor, Rev. Janet Nohavec, is a tutor at Arthur Findlay College and hosts a full schedule of tutors from the AFC at her church in New Jersey, USA.

The Inner Quest Foundation

Victoria, BC V8W 2R9 Canada

1-250-383-1012

www.innerquestfoundation.com

AFC Tutors Brian Robertson and Simon James

An educational center devoted to the ethical and spiritual development of those wishing to pursue the Intuitive Arts.

Fellowships of the Spirit

282 Dale Drive, Lily Dale, NY 14752 USA

(716) 595-2159

www.fellowshipsspirit.org

Both introductory and in depth training in multiple disciplines—mediumship, healing arts & spiritual studies. Many of the classes are taught by Lily Dale mediums and healers.

Kingswells House

Kingswells, Aberdeen, AB15 8PJ Scotland UK

0044 122 427 9457

www.kingswells-house-aberdeen.org.uk

Eileen Davies, Arthur Findlay College Tutor

The house and grounds are used for the progress and encouragement of spiritual awareness for all. Courses, lectures and demonstrations are offered by leading tutors in their field, both in the UK and abroad.

The Monroe Institute

365 Roberts Mountain Road, Faber, VA 22938 USA

(866) 881-3440, 1-434-361-1500

www.monroeinstitute.org

Residential programs enable participants to enter different consciousness states for expanded awareness; exploration of the spirit world; interacting with deceased loved ones, teachers, and guides; remote viewing and out-of-body travel; moving forwards and backwards in time . . .

Online Resources:

SNUi : Spiritualists' National Union International Evidential Mediumship Online Learning.
www.snui.org
Classes, and practice with others worldwide.

Gaia, formerly Gaiam TV.
www.gaia.com (not www.gaiaonline.com)
An online subscription service similar to Netflix but specializing in metaphysical topics, spirituality, personal growth, yoga, mysticism, health, psychic phenomena . . . There are a multitude of excellent interviews with leading thought leaders, authors and teachers, as well as short and full length films, including *Astral City* (or *Our Home*), the Spiritist classic from a book by Chico Xavier.

YouTube Channel:

After Life TV with Bob Olson
youtube.com/user/AfterlifeTVChannel
There are many interesting videos with Bob Olson interviewing mediums, psychics, and people who have contributed to the field of spiritual development.

About the Author

Ruth Shilling, M.M. (Viola Performance), has had a rich and varied career. Beginning as a professional musician—both in Germany and the USA—she later became involved in healing using Therapeutic Touch, sound healing and other subtle energy techniques. The classes she taught in those modalities later moved into an emphasis on spiritual growth and the ability to hear and know the guidance of the Spirit.

While on a second visit to Egypt (1998), she sat in meditation at the Luxor Temple and was asked by the spirits of the place to "bring the people that we may work with them directly." What she understood from that request was that the metaphysical and spiritual tours being offered were basically using Egypt as a backdrop for the teachings of the guest speakers on those tours. What the spirits of the place wanted was to work directly with the spiritual seekers who came to the temples. They even suggested an itinerary that would enable this!

Ruth answered the call and created the **All One World Egypt Tours** company. More than 50 tours have resulted from this alliance and the spirits of the place have taught many, including Ruth herself, during those encounters.

Another tap on the shoulder from Spirit came with an idea of how to help people manifest more of what they want in life by using the easy, free and childlike state that comes about when we are coloring designs. This resulted in the *"Color It True" Adult Coloring Books* series. Each of these is a collection of mandala designs with embedded symbolism to facilitate manifesting, powering up affirmations, or sending positive energies and prayers to those we love. The open space in the center of each design creates a place to focus the intent of the person who is coloring the designs.

The inspiration for the **Through a Medium's Eyes** series of books is described in the introduction (page vii). Hopefully the ideas, experiences and stories in this book will inspire you to clarify and enlarge your own visions and perspectives on life.

See Ruth's current activities at all1world.com, Contact her through one of her websites, Facebook pages or at a1w.books@gmail.com.

Websites

- all1world.com : a listing of all Ruth's activities

- spiritualmedium1.com & inspirationalmedium.com :
  Ruth's mediumship activities, including her spoon
  bending classes and other events

- 1worldtours.com : Egypt tours

- successviolin.com : Ruth's violin, viola &
  chamber music playing and teaching

Facebook Pages

These pages can also be viewed by those who are
not Facebook members.

- Facebook.com/ruthshillingmm/
- Facebook.com/inspirationalmedium/
- Facebook.com/spiritworldmessages/
- Facebook.com/mediumshipinfo/
- Facebook.com/1worldtours/
- Facebook.com/EgyptGodsGoddesses/
- Facebook.com/SinaiDesert/
- Facebook.com/successviolin/
- Facebook.com/flowofwellbeing/
- Facebook.com/RuthsReviews/

Blog

- flowofwellbeing.wordpress.com

Additional Books by Ruth Shilling

Color It True: Adult Coloring Books that Draw Good Things to You!

· *Marvelous Manifestation Mandalas*
   ISBN 978-0-9771991-1-6
· *Magnetic Manifestation Mandalas*
   ISBN 978-0-9771991-2-3
· *Miraculous Manifestation Mandalas*
   ISBN 978-0-9771991-3-0
· *Angelic Manifestation Mandalas*
   ISBN 978-0-9771991-4-7
· *Abundance Manifestation Mandalas*
   ISBN 978-0-9771991-5-4

Violin Success Series

· *SUCCESS with the Violin and Life: Strategies, Techniques & Tips for Learning Quickly & Doing Well.*   ISBN 978-0-9771991-0-9
· *Playing the Violin & Viola with VIBRATO* (ebook).
· *TONE: Violin & Viola Bowing Techniques for a Rich, Satisfying Sound* (ebook).

SINAI: *The Desert & Bedouins of South Sinai's Central Regions.* Palm Press, Cairo, Egypt, 2004
   ISBN 978-9-7750895-2-6
Contains more than 100 full-color photos of the Sinai and the Bedouin people who live there.

Through a Medium's Eyes Series

Rev. B. Anne Gehman
Volume 1

Rev. Carol Gasber
Volume 2

Mavis Pittilla
Volume 3

Neal Rzepkowski, MD
Volume 4

Rev. Simon James
Volume 5

Rev. Brian Robertson
Volume 6

And more to come!

Made in the USA
San Bernardino, CA
02 October 2016